The media's watching Vault!
Here's a sampling of our coverage.

"Unflinching, fly-on-the-wall reports... No one gets past company propaganda to the nitty-gritty inside dope better than these guys."
— *Knight-Ridder newspapers*

"Best way to scope out potential employers...Vault has sharp insight into corporate culture and hiring practices."
— *Yahoo! Internet Life*

"Vault has become a de facto Internet outsourcer of the corporate grapevine."
— *Fortune*

"For those hoping to climb the ladder of success, [Vault's] insights are priceless."
— *Money.com*

"Another killer app for the Internet."
— *New York Times*

"If only the company profiles on the top sites would list the 'real' information... Sites such as Vault do this, featuring insights and commentary from employees and industry analysts."
— *The Washington Post*

"A rich repository of information about the world of work."
— *Houston Chronicle*

VAULT
> the insider career network™

send us your
business plan,
and we'll send you
$50,000.

well, **almost.**

The Carrot Capital Business Plan Challenge rewards the best and brightest collegiate and graduate students for their creativity and innovation in developing winning business plans. Got a great idea for a business? Enter and you could be one of 24 winners to share $100,000 in cash prizes, with the first place team receiving $50,000 *plus* funding for the business! See our website for official rules and dates.

www.**UpToTheChallenge**.com

Forbes

(Principal Sponsor)   (Corporate Sponsors)

VAULT CAREER GUIDE TO
VENTURE CAPITAL

Increase your T/NJ Ratio
(Time to New Job)

Use the Internet's most targeted job search tools for finance professionals.

Vault Finance Job Board

The most comprehensive and convenient job board for finance professionals. Target your search by area of finance, function, and experience level, and find the job openings that you want. No surfing required.

VaultMatch Resume Database

Vault takes match-making to the next level: post your resume and customize your search by area of finance, experience and more. We'll match job listings with your interests and criteria and e-mail them directly to your in-box.

VAULT
> the insider career network™

VAULT CAREER GUIDE TO
VENTURE CAPITAL

BY JAMES CURRIER AND ANITA KAPADIA

For information about permission to reproduce selections from this book, contact Vault Inc., P.O. Box 1772, New York, New York 10011-1772, (212) 366-4212.

Library of Congress CIP Data is available.

ISBN 1-58131-131-1

Printed in the United States of America

Acknowledgments

Vault would like to take the time to acknowledge the assistance and support of Matt Doull, Ahmad Al-Khaled, Lee Black, Eric Ober, Hollinger Capital, Tekbanc, New York City Investment Fund, American Lawyer Media, Globix, Ingram, Hoover's, Glenn Fischer, Mark Hernandez, Ravi Mhatre, Tom Phillips, Carter Weiss, Ken Cron, Ed Somekh, Isidore Mayrock, Zahi Khouri, Sana Sabbagh, Esther Dyson and other Vault investors, as well as our loving families and friends.

Special thanks to Ravi and Carter for their valuable input for the 2002 edition of the Guide. Thanks also to Marcy Lerner, Robert Schipano and Ed Shen.

Looking for a new challenge? The Vault Finance Job Board has
thousands of top jobs for all experience levels. Visit www.vault.com.

VAULT   xi

Introduction

The venture capital field sure has changed since the go-go Internet days of 1999, when it seemed that any business plan with a .com attached to it (even some .nets) could get funding in the millions of dollars. Needless, to say, those days are over — but that doesn't mean that the field of venture capital is defunct. Venture capital firms are being more selective about deals — instead of competing for any half-likely business investment prospect, they are scrutinizing each and every deal that comes across their desks. One venture capitalist has funded four plans in 2001 — out of 360 that made it to the review process.

Don't get us wrong — venture capital firms still have money to invest. The National Venture Capital Association reported U.S. venture capital funds raised $26.4 billion in the first half of 2001. But now that the tech market has cooled off, good judgment in choosing investment opportunities is paramount. In addition, venture capital firms are less likely to invest in early-stage companies (little baby startups), preferring more mature and stable investment opportunities.

A history of VC

Traditionally, individuals, families, or groups of people in tightly-knit communities have invested money in private companies in the U.S. In the 1960s, there were a few wealthy individuals in California who took to investing their money in early stage technology companies. These people were "angels." Returns on investments were excellent. Angels began to systematically search for and invest in companies. In 1971, three of these successful angels raised additional funds from other rich individuals and institutions and placed the money in the early "venture capital funds."

On the East Coast in the late 50s/early 60s a few formal venture investment firms began to arise. One such pioneering firm was American Research & Development Corp., envied for its investment in Digital Equipment Corp.

Venture capital firms suffered a temporary downturn in 1974, when the stock market crashed and investors were naturally wary of this new kind of investment fund. In 1975, only one venture capital fund raised money, but that was the same year Tandem Computer took $1 million from a venture capital firm. Returns were tremendous for the few firms in the business in the late 1970s.

The Federal government lent a helping hand in the form of legislation through this period. In 1978, the government changed the pension plan rules under ERISA (the Employee Retirement Income Security Act), making it possible for pension funds to invest in alternative (and potentially higher risk) asset classes such as venture capital firms. Pension funds represented billions of dollars in capital, so an allocation of even 1 percent of funds represented an enormous increase in the pool of money available to venture capitalists. The industry raised $750 million in 1978.

In 1979, capital gains taxes were reduced from 49 percent to 28 percent, so anyone making profits from investing in venture capital firms, or any venture capital firms making profits from investing in private companies, had to pay less taxes. In 1981, the capital gains tax was further reduced from 28 percent to 20 percent.

Then came 1983 — the year of excess. The stock market peaked and there were over 100 initial public offerings for the first time in U.S. history. That year venture capital investments jumped to a total of $4 billion. Some of 1983's funding went to newly founded companies that are today's largest and most prominent firms such as Apple Computer and Intel.

Due to the excess of IPOs and the inexperience of many venture capital fund managers, VC returns were very low through the 1980s. In 1991, disbursements from the venture capital firms to their investors hit a 10-year low. VC firms retrenched, working hard to make their portfolio companies successful. The work paid off, and returns began climbing back up.

But venture capitalists couldn't take full credit for the turnaround. Macroeconomic forces helped. In the mid-to-late 1980s, interest rates were relatively high, and the price/earnings ratios in the public markets were low. Ten years later, interest rates were low, and P/Es were very high (by historical averages). Pension funds grew dramatically. In 1987, U.S. pension funds held approximately $2.5 trillion. By 1997, that number reached $7 trillion.

The booming economy made pension fund managers more comfortable allocating up to 4 percent of their capital into alternative assets. The U.S. stock market had its greatest run-up in history between 1991 and early 2000. Mutual fund assets grew from $1 trillion in 1990 to over $6 trillion in 1999.

The rate of M&A activity increased dramatically in the late 1990s, creating more opportunities for small, venture-backed companies to exit (cash out) at high prices. After the stock market correction that began in April 2000 the number of venture-backed M&A transactions dropped for several quarters but began to rise again during the first half of 2001. Nevertheless, the value of these venture-backed M&A transactions, while still respectable, is down several-fold from 2000 to 2001.

Venture capital firms taking portfolio companies public in 1999 and 2000 experienced record returns. In general, 1999 and 2000 were boom years for IPOs, and venture-backed firms were particularly prominent. In 2000, 258, or nearly half, of newly public companies were backed by venture capitalists according to the National Venture Capital Association. Not surprisingly, the first half of 2001 has seen only 21 venture-backed IPOs. On average, these companies have done well in the public markets. Venture capitalists were greatly rewarded for their efforts in funding new enterprises. According to Venture Economics, as of March 30th 2001, the return (IRR) for all stages of venture capital funds for one year was -6.7%, for three years was 55.7% and for 20 years was 19%. The venture capital industry is a very cyclical industry. Many industry observers believed 1999/2000 would be the high point before a decline in rates of return; that turned out to be the case. In 1984, 45 new venture capital firms were formed and a long decline in returns and capital raised began. The number of new VCs declined every year through 1991, when the industry actually saw 17 more VC firms go out of business than were formed. In 2000, the industry netted approximately 200 new firms. As evidence to the industry's staying power, approximately 50 new firms were raised in the turbulent first half of 2001.

Looking for a new challenge? The Vault Finance Job Board has thousands of top jobs for all experience levels. Visit www.vault.com.

VAULT   3

The Scoop

The Financial Industry and Venture Capital

Where does VC fit into the world of finance? The financial industry can be divided into two general segments: the buy-side and the sell-side. Sell-side refers to those financial firms that have services to sell, such as investment banks, brokerages, and commercial banks.

For instance, when a large company wants to sell stock on the public stock exchanges, an investment bank's corporate finance department handles the legal, tax, and accounting affairs of the transaction as well as the sale of those securities to institutional or individual investors. For providing these services, the investment bank receives a fee (between 2 percent and 10 percent of the money raised by selling stock). An investment banking firm's primary motivation is to sell such services, characterizing them as sell-siders.

Brokerages are paid a fee for the service they provide of buying and selling stocks. Commercial banks are paid for managing deposit accounts, making and then managing loans, etc. Again, they sell these services, so they are sell-side firms.

Venture capital firms, on the other hand, are on the buy-side because they control a pool or fund of money to spend on buying an equity interest in, or assets of, operating companies.

Buy-side firms make money when they sell their equity to another private investor, a corporation (trade sale) or to the public markets for more money than they paid. Descriptions of each segment of the buy-side are included below. Keep in mind that these definitions are intended to be very general in nature and that many buy-side organizations cross organizational boundaries.

Angels

These are wealthy individuals who normally invest between $50,000 and $3 million in exchange for equity in a young company. Angels sit on the board of directors and contribute experience and contacts, guiding young companies through the difficult initial stages of growth. Angels can be doctors, lawyers, former investors, though increasingly they are former

Looking for a new challenge? The Vault Finance Job Board has thousands of top jobs for all experience levels. Visit www.vault.com.

VAULT 5

entrepreneurs. Microsoft co-founder and multi-billionaire Paul Allen has made headlines for his angel investing as well as his investments through his VC firm, Vulcan Partners. Intel co-founder Andy Grove has made angel investments in numerous companies, including Oncology.com. Given the large number of new companies seeking funding as well as the rise in the number of wealthy individuals, in recent years the industry has seen the emergence of angel groups. These investor alliances create more structure for angel investors. Perhaps the best-known group of angels is Silicon Valley's "Band of Angels," a group of about 150 people who meet monthly to consider pleas for venture capital investments from entrepreneurs. Angels are often involved with hiring, strategy, the raising of additional capital, and fundamental operating decisions. Angels also have their own issues. Collectively, angel investors are also one of the first sources of private equity to dry up when public markets fall or macroeconomic conditions deteriorate. Many of these individuals have a lower tolerance for losses, which is compounded by their generally lower position in the capital structure. Their equity rarely has the same level of preferences or security demanded by later stage investors. They also tend to have much smaller pools of capital to work from. Though angels, of course, expect a significant return on their investment, they are also thrill-seekers of a sort – motivated by getting close to the excitement of a new venture.

High net worth private placements

Sell-side companies, such as investment banks, may organize a group of very wealthy individuals, corporations, asset management firms, and/or pension funds to make a direct investment into a private company. The amount raised from these sources is typically between $5 million and $50 million. In essence, the sell-side company enables investors to invest in the venture capital asset class.

While these transactions may include a traditional venture fund as part of the round, in many cases they do not. The downside is that 1) the company may not benefit from the expertise of the venture capital firm, and 2) the sell-side company takes a fee for its services, typically between 2 and 10 percent of capital raised.

Asset management firms

This group includes a diverse group of limited partnerships and corporations that manage between $5 million and $20 billion and focus on diversified investment strategies, typically with public instruments including stocks, bonds, commodities, currencies, etc. They rarely invest in private companies, due to the large amount of time required to find and execute a private investment, as well as the ongoing commitment of time to monitor a private investment.

Leveraged buyout firms

These are limited partnerships or corporations that take over private or public firms using their own capital as equity, combined with debt (leverage) financing from third-party banks. After acquiring a company, the LBO firm normally changes management and the direction of the firm, or may divide and sell its assets. The size of LBOs ranges from a few million to many billions of dollars. These firms look and behave very much like venture capital firms, but their investments differ in size and purpose. Both LBOs and VCs fall under the umbrella descriptor "Private Equity."

Hedge funds

These are limited partnerships or corporations that buy and sell public market instruments including stocks, bonds, commodities, currencies, etc. These firms take bets on market fluctuations and are often considered high risk/high return investors. The size of these funds ranges from a few million to several billion dollars.

Trading

Sell-side companies such as merchant banks, commercial banks and investment banks have trading departments that control and invest huge sums of money into public markets. These groups also take relatively risky bets on market fluctuations.

Looking for a new challenge? The Vault Finance Job Board has
thousands of top jobs for all experience levels. Visit www.vault.com.

VAULT   7

Stages of Venture Capital Investment

Venture capital firms invest in what could be considered five different stages of a company's growth. Again, these stages are general guidelines, and may sometimes overlap.

Seed

Investment of between $1,000 and $500,000 made in a company's embryonic stage – a handful of people with an idea and little or no revenue.

Start-Up

Investment of between $50,000 and $1 million in private companies that are completing product development and beginning initial marketing.

Early Stage (or First Stage)

An investment of between $500,000 and $15 million made when a company has completed its product but has unimpressive revenues.

Later Stage (or Second Stage)

An investment of between $2 million and $15 million when a firm has product and revenues and has often already taken money from other institutional investors.

Mezzanine (or Third Stage)

An investment of between $2 million and $20 million into a company for a major expansion, generally leading to an initial public offering in three to 18 months.

Bridge

Often, the term "bridge financing" is used to describe a speedy financing of a company that is in trouble and needs some more time to get to a more substantial round of financing.

But sometimes a bridge financing is a bridge to an IPO. In this case, "bridge" refers to an investment of between $2 million and $20 million made three to

12 months before the company goes public. ("Going public" means it issues equity shares for purchase by the public.) Another common way to say "going public" is "IPO" or "initial public offering." The company is typically profitable at this stage (except in the case of Internet companies, which rarely are!).

There are several reasons a company might take on a round of bridge financing just prior to its IPO (when it would presumably raise a lot of money). It might want to bolster its balance sheet in order to be more attractive to investors. The company alternatively might want to snare a prestigious board member/investor, also in order to increase its IPO value. Finally, some companies may want to hedge their bets in case of a failed IPO.

Looking for a new challenge? The Vault Finance Job Board has
thousands of top jobs for all experience levels. Visit www.vault.com.

VAULT   9

The "Capital" in VC

Where do buy-side funds get their money? Most of the money comes from pension funds. Funds are also derived from endowments of non-profit institutions such as universities and museums, foundations, insurance companies, banks, and from wealthy families and individual corporations.

Pension funds are funds set aside by corporations (typically large) for their employees' retirements. The money piles up over the years and can amount to billions of dollars. This money must be invested so that its value will be sufficient to cover the needs of the employees at the time of retirement. To maximize return and minimize risk, the pension money is invested in many places — stocks, bonds, currencies, real estate, and "alternative investments."

Typically, 1 to 5 percent of the total funds are invested into what pension fund managers call "alternative investments," and what we call the "buy-side" firms. Pension fund managers expect higher rates of return (15 to 30 percent) from these alternative asset investments and they understand there is a commensurately higher risk associated with such investments.

The aim of the buy-side firms, including venture capital firms, is to provide high rates of return to their investors. Only by producing high rates of return can buy-side firms continue to raise money and thereby stay in business. Venture capital firms are therefore beholden to the pension funds and endowments. (Following the "golden rule" logic, the venture capital firms tend to have the upper hand with companies into which they invest.)

These power relations don't always hold true. When a venture capital firm produces very high rates of return on a consistent basis, pension funds will compete to invest in it, allowing the venture firm to dictate terms. Venture capital firms may also compete to invest in a particularly hot start-up (perhaps one with a high rate of growth, or one started by a entrepreneur with a track record of success).

How Venture Capital Funds Are Structured

The Traditional Venture Capital Fund

Most venture capital funds are set up as independent Limited Partnerships. The venture capital firm acts as the General Partner (GP) with third-party institutions, investing the bulk of the capital to the fund, acting as Limited Partners (LPs). Funds generally raise anywhere from $10 million to several billion dollars from institutions. The venture fund in turn invests this capital in privately held, high-growth, companies. In 2001 a typical new fund had approximately $200 million in committed capital.

A partnership agreement sets forth the relationship between the GP (the VC firm) and their LPs (investors). The returns of the venture capital fund are distributed back to the LPs as dictated by the partnership agreement, but naturally lean toward the later years of the fund. The reason for the preponderance of partnerships, as opposed to corporations, is the security it gives the VC firm to make long-term decisions. Once an agreement is signed and the capital commitments are made, the LPs are generally stuck with this group of venture professionals for the duration of the partnership (VC funds are generally organized as 10-year partnerships). During the duration of the partnership, the institutional investors cannot remove their capital from the fund at will. Capital is distributed back to investors according to the partnership agreement, unlike a mutual fund where cash invested can be withdrawn at any time. As a result however, the arrangement allows VC firms to act as a relatively reliable pool of risk capital. Plus, VC firms will rarely "go bankrupt." If unsuccessful, they are more likely to be wound down over time without the ability to raise an additional fund.

A typical 10-year venture capital fund may cash flow something like this:

- Year one to four — Initial portfolio company investments are made

- Years three through seven — Follow-on investments are made into the portfolio companies

- Years three through ten — The investments are exited/liquidated.

Looking for a new challenge? The Vault Finance Job Board has thousands of top jobs for all experience levels. Visit www.vault.com.

VAULT 11

A venture capital firm may be managing several individual funds at any given time. The individual funds are distinct entities with their own set of limited partners, although they sometimes overlap across funds. As one might imagine, this creates a pile of issues that we will not try to go into here (if you really want to know how the story of VC partnership ends, both Josh Lerner and Joe Bartlett have leading books on the subject).

Distributions and Carried Interest

Typically, venture capital fund profits are distributed as follows: 80 percent to the limited partners and 20 percent to the general partner (carried interest) after the limited partners have received their initial investment back. During fever-paced period of 1999 and 2000, these percentages adjusted to a 70/30 split for some of the most popular and promising funds raised. To nobody's surprise, 2001 and 2002 funds are having a harder time negotiating a 30 percent carry. There are endless variations on carry, distribution and similar terms. These are ultimately established through negotiations on a case-by-case basis. (See the glossary at the end of this guide for definitions of terms related to the venture capital industry.)

Management Fees

The general partner (VC firm) charges a fee for its role as portfolio manager. This management fee covers the fund's costs such as rent, salaries and keeping the lights on. The fee is usually 1 to 2.5 percent of the assets, or committed capital.

Why is all this important? Because at the end of the day this is how you get paid. That 20 percent of carry is split amongst the employees of the firm at the discretion of the managing or general partners. Compensation will be detailed later.

Corporate Venture Capital Programs

Corporate venture capital programs typically begin as subsidiaries of large corporations (e.g., Intel Capital, GE Equity, TI Ventures, Cisco, Tribune Ventures). These subsidiaries will either make investments that are of "strategic" value to the parent corporation or they will function purely as financial investors capitalizing on the technology, know-how, reputation, and access to capital of the parent. While somewhat controversial, these programs can produce some of the most enviable returns in the industry, and successful programs are often spun off as separate venture funds. Historically, it has been hard for corporate venture capital programs to retain good venture capital professionals and to stay the course when shareholders have a quarter-by-quarter view. Nevertheless it looks as if they will continue to be an increasingly important part of venture capital.

Other Venture Capital Structures

Venture capital firms can be effective with structures other than the ones outlined above. Limited Liability Corporations (LLCs) are an alternative form of structuring a fund, but for our purposes, these function in a similar manner as Limited Partnerships. The venture capital firm meVC is an example of a closed end publicly traded venture fund (while it is too early to tell what their returns will be, they did raise $300M in investment capital).

While there are endless maturations for organizing venture capital firms, atypical structures should set off a red flag for the applicant. "Why are they not a fund?" is the first question that a job-seeker should ask themselves. While many alternative methods of organization have merit, a prospective applicant should be comfortable that the firm has sufficient unencumbered capital and are not just trying to look as if they do.

Looking for a new challenge? The Vault Finance Job Board has
thousands of top jobs for all experience levels. Visit www.vault.com.

VAULT   13

Industry Trends

Because of the technology and Internet boom of the late 1990s, not only have the number of venture capital firms increased dramatically, but the size of the funds they manage has jumped as well. (Whether the number of worthwhile investments has increased proportionately is doubtful.) An increasing number of VC firms have achieved the elite $1 billion+ capital under management mark. Still, even the most elite and successful firms have seen the value of their tech investments dwindle, and some have been wound down.

Organizations and publications such as Venture One, Venture Economics, The National Venture Capital Association and the *Venture Capital Journal* provide a great deal of analysis about the macro trends in the industry. They keep track of how much capital has been invested in VC funds each year, how much was deployed from those funds into companies each year, into which areas of the country and into which industry segments the money was deployed, what the rates of return on those investments have been, and so on.

Traditional venture capital firms are accompanied by the venture capital activity of huge corporations such as Intel, Microsoft, Hewlett-Packard, Adobe, and Motorola. These monoliths have learned how to make minority investments while allowing the invested companies freedom to compete effectively through corporate venture programs and strategic investment groups. It wasn't always thus — in the past, large corporations were reluctant to invest in companies they didn't control, and their VC operations often came and went. The old greenhouse model used by the Baby Bells, Corning, Xerox, IBM and Teradyne has given way to a newer model that closely parallels the investing strategies of the VC firms, and is proving much more successful. Because of the recent downturn in the market, however, many corporations are curtailing their corporate VC investments to some degree.

Venture firms also face competition from angels, the former entrepreneurs who got rich during the last decade of explosive growth in the stock market. (In 1999, for example, Sendmail, a hot start-up, opted to take financing from The Band of Angels instead of some top VC firms.) Like corporate VC programs, angel investment has declined recently as many angels have seen their welath decline significantly.

Organizational changes

The organizational structure of venture capital firms is evolving. In the past few years, VC firms have been employing more associates – sub-partner personnel. (This is a good thing for eager MBAs attempting to enter the competitive venture capital industry.)

Until 1995, most firms had little support other than their own network of professional contacts out in the community. Then companies like Summit Partners, TA Associates, and Battery Ventures built effective, high-return VC firms by relying upon junior level personnel. Associates became experts in niche markets, providing value with the sheer depth of their understanding. Combining deep, narrow knowledge from associates and broad business and strategic knowledge from general partners has proved to be a very effective model.

Another organizational change to VCs has resulted from the trend of venture capital firms to become more proactive in ensuring the success of their investments. Some sizable VCs are adding early stage functional experts to their firms in areas like mergers and acquisitions, executive recruiting, public relations, market research and operations. These in-house personnel allow the venture capital firms to add more value, assert more control over the life of the investment, and increase the possibility that the portfolio companies become bottom-line boons.

Looking for a new challenge? The Vault Finance Job Board has
thousands of top jobs for all experience levels. Visit www.vault.com.
VAULT   15

Getting Hired

An Overview of the Hiring Process

Venture capital remains a hot field, and aspiring venture capitalists have their work cut out for them. But it's not impossible to get hired in this dynamic area.

Your first step should be to identify all possible areas in which you might be able to start a venture capital career. These include:

- Private partnerships and small, incorporated entities (prestigious and sexy, they give the industry its reputation)

- Corporate venture programs or divisions of major corporations (Intel Capital, the VC unit of Intel Corp., has invested over $1 billion.)

- Affiliates of investment banks (J.P. Morgan Chase has a notable VC division)

- Venture leasing companies (they take equity in return for a lower rate on leased equipment or real estate)

- Direct investment activity by insurance companies, pension funds or investment advisory firms

- SBICs (Small Business Investment Corporations). These are privately capitalized venture capital firms, which are eligible to receive federal loans to augment the private funds invested in them. SBICs are privately managed, but are licensed and regulated by the Small Business Administration.

- Funds of Funds (fund structures that primarily invest as limited partners in multiple venture funds) can be a good stepping-stone

- Hedge Funds with established venture capital teams

The next step involves developing the required skill set for a venture capitalist. Some of the skills mentioned here are not required of those in junior positions, but you will be evaluated on your ability to develop these skills over time.

Schmoozing: Schmooze everyone in sight to find deals first or to latch onto hot companies. Schmoozing also comes in handy when you're doing due

Looking for a new challenge? The Vault Finance Job Board has thousands of top jobs for all experience levels. Visit www.vault.com.

VAULT   17

diligence on a company and its market – you must find the sources of information you need and then extract the appropriate information. A good network is a big success factor in any industry, but this is doubly true for venture capital. Building a big Rolodex either in a geographic region or an industry is a must.

Consulting: You need to be able to give superior strategic advice to your portfolio companies in areas such as hiring and firing, technical strategy, sales execution, distribution, growth strategy, and product mix. Your advice is one of the big "value-added" features of having a venture firm as an investor. Previous work experience as a consultant can't hurt, but is often not enough by itself.

Financial knack: A venture capitalist advises an entrepreneur on financial strategy. This requires corporate finance knowledge. A deep knowledge of accounting and hands-on experience with mergers and acquisitions are of particular value. The VC works with I-bankers when an IPO rolls around and manages large amounts of money. Excel is, as always, your friend.

Industry expertise: Because you will invest in the cutting-edge companies of whatever industry you are focused on (telecom, software, biotech, consumer products, retail, health service, etc) you need to be a player in that industry to get credibility. You need to know the other hot companies, top managers, the industry history and lore, and the latest rumors and trends. This kind of knowledge is necessary to give superior advice in competitive positioning, alliances and partnerships, and executive hiring.

Good judgement: Either you're born with it or you learn it by trial and error. Either way, it's necessary for savvy investment decisions.

Where Do You Start?

Disclaimer: The titles used in venture capital do not necessarily correspond to common investment banking definitions, though they seem to be moving that direction. To muddy the water a little further, each venture capital firms will apply titles differently. An applicant should pay extra attention to the actual job description in venture capital.

Analyst/Associate — entry level

If you are coming out of college and have little experience in the working world, this is your starting spot in the world of VC. This position is called associate or sometimes analyst, depending on the firm. Be aware that many firms do not hire straight out of undergrad (because hands-on experience is such an important component to the business). Display some entrepreneurial activity in your background and some type-A, oddball experience – a pilot's license, racing a sailboat to Bermuda, running an investment club of students, starting a boxer shorts company, and so forth. Most importantly, you need to be fun, confident, quantitatively skilled and willing to work hard.

Associate/Senior Associate/Principal/V.P. — partner track

If you have industry experience (e.g., telecommunications, medical devices, consumer products) and/or have your MBA, this is the position you're shooting for. This position is often considered "partner track." An MBA is almost always a prerequisite. The most important attribute is to show good judgment and impeccable schmoozing talents.

Junior Partner/General Partner

This position enables you to make investment decisions. It is only conferred on those who have very deep industry experience or those who have shown they can make such decisions at another firm. The good news is it is not uncommon for serial entrepreneurs and successful industry players to move directly into these positions. Venture capital is a business often entered into later in one's career. A good set of golf clubs is a prerequisite.

Looking for a new challenge? The Vault Finance Job Board has thousands of top jobs for all experience levels. Visit www.vault.com.

VAULT   19

Managing Partner

Raise your own fund and start a venture capital firm!

Figure out your probability of success before you start spending hundreds of hours banging on doors. Look at the numbers. There aren't many positions available, and the ones that exist are hard to find. Why?

- The venture capital industry is small. It is made up of only several hundred small firms (each consisting of between two and 40 people). People rarely leave venture capital once they're in. It's too much fun spending money on the latest ideas, working with highly motivated and intelligent people and the latest ideas, and making lots of money. It's also hard for a venture capitalist to transfer into more regimented careers.

- The old boys network is in full force in this corner of the economy. The portion of partners with degrees from Harvard and Stanford is very high.

- The demand for positions is so great that the openings are often filled through networking and not publicly advertised.

How big is the venture capital industry? The number changes depending on what you call a "Venture Capital" firm. The National Venture Capital Association estimates about 8,000 VC professionals. We came up with the following estimates for the number of positions nationwide in the industry.

Analysts/Associates (entry level): 750-1,000

Senior Associates/VP (partner track): 1,000-1,500

Partners: 4,000

Firms: 700-750

The most authoritative source for companies of the types listed above is *Pratt's Guide to Venture Capital Sources* (published by Thomson Financial). You should check it out in the reference section of your local library. However, if you call these firms, you'll find out that a fair number are either gone or winding down. And, some firms aren't listed in Pratt's because they are new and haven't been listed yet. And some firms simply don't want to advertise themselves at all.

Estimating the senior associate and analyst/associate numbers is difficult because the turnover at these positions is rapid (two to four years). Our educated guess is shown above. The number of "non-partner professionals" in VC firms has in recent years grown by approximately 8 to 15 percent per year, but may be flat or down for 2001 and 2002.

Targeting the Firm You Want

The most prominent and traditional venture firms are located in the San Francisco area and Boston. New York tends to have later stage, lower-technology firms with more capital deployed per transaction, and, as a venture capital city, follows closely behind the top two. Washington, D.C., Philadelphia, and Los Angeles are the next tier (along with Texas and the Southeast) but are also very strong. Most larger cities have at least a few firms that place themselves in the venture capital category.

Don't overlook the less prominent, less competitive geographic areas with high entrepreneurial growth like Minnesota, North Carolina, Utah, Colorado, Washington state, Pittsburgh, Atlanta, and Chicago. The growth of these venture capital communities is not far behind the rise of the entrepreneurs, and you can get in on the ground floor. Other reasons to check these locations out include:

- It might be easier to get a job
- The day-to-day job is the same or better (because you'll end up having more responsibility)
- Quality of life will be better because of lower pressure and less constraints on your behavior

Don't just target the high-prestige, private funds. Look at university funds, SBICs and venture divisions of corporations. If your ultimate goal is to work for the better known firms, your best bet might be to pursue the lower profile firms, prove yourself for a few years, and then move to the big leagues later.

On the other hand, working at the most prestigious firms gives you:

- More job opportunities down the road
- Higher name recognition
- A better platform from which to meet people in the industries you follow
- A front row seat on how the best minds in the business think

Looking for a new challenge? The Vault Finance Job Board has
thousands of top jobs for all experience levels. Visit www.vault.com.

VAULT   21

Getting the Interview

VC firms are inundated with requests for interviews and informational interviews. The time of venture capitalists is precious. If a VC firm lets it be known they have a single summer internship available, they can expect 300 resumes from people at the top 10 business schools. Now that you're more aware of what you are up against, here's a glint of hope – as a whole, venture capital firms are always hiring.

So what can you do? Network. Ultimately, networking and schmoozing is the key to a job search in every industry, but it is even more so in the VC industry. Building contacts in the industry is key to finding out about jobs and getting an interview. It helps to have a strong recommendation from someone the VC respects.

The other way to get an interview is to have deep industry experience. This takes a few years, so it's not for the impatient.

Another way to up your chances at an interview – do your research. Target a niche attractive to VC firms. Read the trade press or go to a large trade show and catch up on the buzz.

By far he best way to approach a venture capital firm is via a simple introduction to one of the professionals. "Johnny Trustworthy suggested I contact you about…", will make a big difference. Part of your job should be finding people who are in a position to make this introduction. All VCs work with lots of lawyers, bankers, portfolio companies, and boards of directors. Poll your network to see who might know at the right people at these outfits as well as the VC firms themselves.

Then get access to VentureOne (a Reuters product) or VentureXpert (a Thomson Financial product). These databases are very expensive, but you should be able to get access at a local business school or at a friend's investment bank or venture capital firm.

VentureOne and VentureXpert chronicle investments reported by venture capital firms across the U.S. They give you the name of the company invested, which VC firms made the investment, how much was invested, and a short description of what the company does. By studying the information, you may glean an indication of what are currently considered hot investments. You might also start to see patterns where certain names of firms are repeatedly attached to companies that interest you. This info will help you focus your list of preferred venture capital firms.

Then hit the Web to find out about each of the companies in that space, the VCs that invested in them, and the opinions of journalists who write about the niche. Develop your own ideas about the market and find other private companies that haven't yet attracted investors. Trade shows are among the best way to research companies. Once you have developed ideas backed up by research, you can approach and impress a VC.

Kauffman Fellowship

Another way to get a post-MBA job in VC is the Kauffman Fellowship (www.kauffmanfellows.org). The $1 billion Kauffman Foundation was created by Ewing Marion Kauffman in 1992 to support youth development programs and to accelerate entrepreneurship in America. The fellowship is one of the foundation's innovative programs. Its mission is to increase the number of well-trained venture capitalists in the U.S. by placing and paying for top candidates to work as associates in prestigious venture capital firms. It is an excellent program, and has been responsible for a significant percentage of the next generation of venture capitalists over the last few years. Kauffman fellows now represent their own alumni group within the VC industry and use that network to help other alums.

Acing the interview

As mentioned before, VC firms are always looking for people. When a firm finds someone they really like, they can afford to hire them. The simple reason is that the "right" person will add a lot more value than they cost.

So who is the "right" person? As it turns out, the right person for a VC firm can have almost any background – degrees ranging from psychology to English, and industry experience from non-profit and government to management consulting, investment banking, business operations, and of course, entrepreneurial activities.

Then what are venture capital firms looking for? An intangible quality – a winning personality and keen business judgment. VC firms are tiny compared to most other professional outfits. They are high-pressure partnerships where the alchemy of strong personalities becomes critical to the

Looking for a new challenge? The Vault Finance Job Board has
thousands of top jobs for all experience levels. Visit www.vault.com.

VAULT 23

success of the firm. VC candidates often interview with every professional at a firm – and typically, everyone in the firm has veto power.

On the other hand, VC interviews are not tricky. Generally, there are no brainteasers or case questions. A VC interview is a chance for venture capitalists to get a sense of you, the same way they do when meeting with entrepreneurs. That's how VCs make investment decisions – by gut instinct. Hiring is no different.

As a result, the interviews are often very personal in nature. You may be asked questions about your family, your friends, your former co-workers and bosses, even your romantic relationships. The VC wants to know if he/she can bear to work closely with you and depend on you for million dollar decisions. Pay attention to your meetings with analysts and associates when interviewing. They are often just as important, if not more so, than the partners.

The Questions

Questions in VC interviews typically fall into three categories: questions about your expertise, questions about the VC process, and personality/fit questions.

Expertise questions

1   What are the major trends in your industry?

First, be able to explain the big picture. "My industry built overcapacity over the last six years, so a wave of consolidation is beginning." "Explosive growth and competition for technical talent has made the business unprofitable, so we are looking overseas." This shows you can frame market forces in simple and understandable ways.

Second, explain subtle trends that would only be apparent to an observant insider. "There was an assumption in the industry, based on macro price competition, that the customer didn't want higher prices. Turns out consumers believed that higher prices indicated quality, so the companies positioned in the upper tier have fared better." "Four of the six competitors didn't pay close enough attention to the standards bodies and wasted two years building software that won't be compatible with the next generation databases. They're in trouble and they don't even know it yet." This sort of insight shows you get how things really work.

2   Can you explain why your former company took the path they did?

More insight, more demonstration that you "get it." "They said it was a strategic alliance, but in reality, it appears the Board of Directors chose the path of least resistance."

3   When you did that project, did you use a certain technology?

What did you think of it? Review all the projects and jobs on your resume. What specific details did you observe and think about during or after the project. How did you make your decisions and why?

Looking for a new challenge? The Vault Finance Job Board has thousands of top jobs for all experience levels. Visit www.vault.com.

VAULT   25

4   **What companies in your industry might make interesting investments?**

This is the end game for VCs. Always have an answer for this question.

Process questions

1   **How would you value an investment?**

The idea is to value it as low as possible and still have the entrepreneur take the money and give you a seat on the board. Say you would use several methods and then triangulate on a number. That number would serve as an anchor around which you would begin discussions with the entrepreneurs.

Begin by putting an upper bound on the valuation by estimating the maximum potential exit valuation for a company and then calculating the maximum price the firm could pay and still get their desired return. That desired return is typically 40 percent per year, or 10 times the invested capital over a reasonable period, such as five years.

The Discounted Cash Flow (DCF) method can only be used on later stage companies with significant profit history and relatively predictable growth plans. Price earnings multiples from comparable public companies is a fair method, but not the best. A third and more common way VCs hone in on valuation is to look at comparable private equity investments made by other VCs in similar firms.

2   **When you evaluate a business plan, what's the most critical element you look for?**

The answer is management – the brains behind the operation. The market opportunity is a good fallback answer.

3   **Why do you want to work at a venture capital firm?**

Do not mention trendiness or money.

4   Would you want to invest in companies geographically near or far from our offices?

You want to invest near the VC offices to make monitoring and supporting the company easier. You would try to increase returns by giving each invested company more attention and thus an increased chance of succeeding. Early stage investments especially need assistance.

On the other hand, it's worthwhile to search for lower valuations on good companies in faraway regions underserved by competing venture capital firms.

5   What investment areas do you find interesting?

Do some research on a niche within the investment landscape of the firm. It will take hours of reading in the library, but should give you a differentiated interview and show you are truly interested in venture capital. The VC may disagree with you, but as long as you have good reasons for your opinion, and can show them you can disagree confidently and constructively, you score big.

6   Do you have any questions for me?

This is your big chance to differentiate and you must have some killer questions to show you're a critical thinker. The best place to start is to ask questions about the near-term evolution of the firm.

Learn about firm's portfolio companies and which partner sits on which board. Learn the histories of the companies. You can find out most of this from the Web and trade press. It also helps to talk to other VCs. Discover companies the venture capital firm (probably) regrets not investing in. Asking about a missed opportunity shows you know that all firms err – and shows that you've done your research.

Looking for a new challenge? The Vault Finance Job Board has
thousands of top jobs for all experience levels. Visit www.vault.com.

VAULT   27

Personality/Fit Questions

1   Where do you want to be in five years?

If the position you are interviewing for is pre-MBA, express a desire to attend business school and be in a position to work in the venture capital industry somewhere. Many firms are worried about making promises to young professionals they can't keep if the person doesn't fit into a partner track position later, so they might be more comfortable if you don't say, "I want to be a partner at your firm."

If the position is a partner track position, you should probably want to suggest you are looking for a place as a partner in five years, preferably at their firm.

2   Would you ever want to be an entrepreneur?

If you are a pre-MBA candidate, it's fine to say yes. Most VC types have entrepreneurial leanings and vice versa. However, for a partner-track candidate, this is a dangerous question. If a VC firm is going to give you a coveted partner-track position, they want you to stay in the firm and make them a lot of money.

3   What will you do if you don't get a job here or in the venture capital industry?

Say you'd work on leads with other VC firms, or with related businesses like investment banks, market research firms, or small companies that might interest VCs. The keys here are 1) to be excited about other jobs that are similar to the job you are interviewing for, and 2) to have other options. VCs instinctively value something higher if there's competition for it (and that includes you). That said, prioritize venture capital.

4   **What did you like about your old job and why did you leave?**

Be sure you know the answer to this. The answer to this question should indicate your strengths and why VC is the right industry for you at this point. Be clear about why you are moving on, but don't complain excessively about your previous job.

5   **What's the thing you are most proud of?**

Have some great stories prepared from the "personal" section at the bottom of your resume.

Looking for a new challenge? The Vault Finance Job Board has
thousands of top jobs for all experience levels. Visit www.vault.com.

VAULT   29

On the Job

Training

Around the industry, one often hears that "venture capital is an apprenticeship business" – it needs to be learned on the job. (That's why there are very few formal training programs at venture capital firms.) A common saying in VC is: "It takes $4 million to make a venture capitalist." This means beginners often start with about $4 million in a series of investments that fail before gaining the insight to make a good investment.

Judgement is the name of the game in the business. No one can define it, but venture capitalists claim they have it and that they know it when they see it in others. VC firms pick people who have judgement or have the potential to learn judgement, and let them hang around to get a feeling, a sense, and an awareness, of how to create wealth. That means "training" in a venture firm is limited only by your curiosity and the willingness of the partners to allow access to the deal process.

What you do

Associates have three main functions at VC firms: 1) sourcing deals, 2) performing due diligence on potential investments, and 3) supporting the portfolio companies.

What associates do when sourcing deals

- Consult with analysts at I-banks or market research firms
- Attend trade shows
- Read trade press releases
- Talk with entrepreneurs
- Probe carefully during due diligence calls
- Gossip with other VCs
- Talk to accountants and lawyers
- Surf the Internet for research
- Think strategically/brainstorm about potential opportunities
- Attend investment conferences where companies seeking capital present to an audience of investors
- Build a strong network of ongoing qualified deal flow.

Looking for a new challenge? The Vault Finance Job Board has thousands of top jobs for all experience levels. Visit www.vault.com.

VAULT   31

Performing due diligence on potential investments

- Talk to customers

- Research and talk to the competition

- Find and interview industry experts about the market/competition/trends

- Bring in technical consultants to evaluate the technology

- Perform management background checks

- Bring in lawyers to review contracts/patents/licenses etc.

- Bring in accounting consultants to verify financials (or roll up your own sleeves)

- Talk with previous investors

- Spend time with management and at the company looking for red flags

Supporting portfolio companies

- Research and strategic planning

- Attend Board of Directors meetings

- Help locate and screen potential additions to a company's management team

- Convince new recruits that they should work with your portfolio company

- Support the management team (can be anything from being a friend to "hand-holding")

- Negotiate and work with I-bankers

- Negotiate and work with acquirers of the company

- Raise more money from other equity sources

- Negotiate with banks for debt financing

- Report to the rest of your VC firm on changes, problems and triumphs

- Help acquire other companies

As an associate, your first order of duty will be to support the partners and leverage their time. Remember, they have hired you so they can deploy more money in profitable investments. For the privilege of the apprenticeship, you are expected to create a lot more value for the firm than your compensation would suggest.

Early stage – deal sourcing

In an early stage venture firm, you will be expected to source deals. You need to reach out into the world and bring investment opportunities to the firm. This amounts to calling and visiting companies to ascertain their attractiveness and interest in raising capital. This isn't as easy as it sounds! Deal sourcers will go to trade shows, talk with their networks of friends, read the trade press, work with other VCs, attend local networking events and investment conferences, read unsolicited business plans, and talk to portfolio company managers. There are hundreds of deal sourcers at work at any given time – and being the first VC to a company matters.

When sourcing deals, schmoozing is key. Any acquaintance or friend might give you the next lead on a company. VC associates must build personal relationships with business partners to up the level of trust and interdependence.

Late stage – due diligence

Associates support partners in due diligence analysis of an investment opportunity. Later stage companies are normally no secret (they're typically large enough to have attracted press and other attention). The trick is not to uncover the investment opportunity, but to get a company to take your money. Consequently, the partner is usually the one to source later stage deals. Associates perform due diligence: building spreadsheets and running sensitivity analyses, calling references, investigating competitors, validating legal contracts, visiting remote locations, coordinating with other investors, and so on.

Ultimately, associates and partners must decide how best to use the most precious resource: time. Which markets to research? Which company to work on? Which entrepreneur to call back? Which spreadsheet model to build? Which references to call? Which trip to take, which meeting to make? As an apprentice venture capitalist, associates must make decisions all day long. Many of those decisions have to do with which potential assignments to pursue. A venture firm is responsible for the money in its fund, and the clock is ticking.

Looking for a new challenge? The Vault Finance Job Board has thousands of top jobs for all experience levels. Visit www.vault.com.

VAULT   33

A Day in the Life of A Venture Capitalist

7:00   Arrive at the office.

7:01   Read *The Wall Street Journal*, paying careful attention to the Marketplace section covering your industry focus.

7:20   Read trade press and notice four companies you haven't seen before. Check your firm's internal database to see if someone else on your team has contacted the companies. Search the Internet to find out more. Of the four companies you find, only one holds your interest. Send yourself an e-mail as a reminder to call them during business hours.

7:45   Clip out some interesting articles and put them in the in-boxes of other associates or partners with a note explaining why you found the information interesting. The other members of your firm have more expertise in the areas covered by the articles. You stay and talk for a few minutes with each of the people in their offices, exchanging the latest word about the people and technology you follow.

8:00   Respond to e-mails or voice mails from the day before. People you are communicating with are primarily entrepreneurs, other VCs, and personal acquaintances.

9:00   You attend a meeting with a group of entrepreneurs who want to make their pitch. You read the business plan for five minutes. One general partner (GP) sits in with you. The other GP, who planned to be there, cannot make it because he has a conference call with a portfolio company facing some challenges. The computer projecting the entrepreneur's presentation crashes, so you have to take their paper version of their presentation and work with your assistant to make four photocopies before the meeting can proceed.

        During the 10-minute delay, the partner talks with the team informally, and learns more about the opportunity than he or she would in any one-hour presentation. You sit politely through the presentation, and identify the three critical issues facing the company.

During the question and answer phase, you think of how to politely extract more information about those three issues, all the while evaluating whether you would want to work with this team or not.

In the end, you decide to make some calls to gather more information about the market, or a competitor, but you feel that there's a very low probability you would ever invest. You wish you could just kill the deal, but the management team is reasonable (though not great), the customer need they have identified may actually exist (you don't know first-hand, so you will need to call around), and you may learn something by taking it to the next step. Plus, in the back of your mind, you know the market for good deals is very competitive, and you don't want to reject a deal too quickly.

11:00   Phone the people who called during your meeting. These people include entrepreneurs, analysts, other VC's, and your lunch appointment. You find out from another VC that the company you almost invested in two months ago just got funded by a competing firm. You wonder if you made a mistake. You find out from an entrepreneur you were hoping to back that he wants his son to be a co-founder and owner of the firm. You abandon all hope. You learn from an analyst that AT&T has decided to stop its trial of a new technology because it doesn't work, which creates an opportunity for companies with a alternative solution. You happen to know about two small companies, one in Boston, one in Denver, that have alternative solutions. You make a note to yourself to call them back to get a status report.

12:30   Lunch with an executive recruiter. This person is very experienced in finding management talent in your area of expertise. You have kept in touch with her over the years, and try to see her every quarter to hear the latest buzz and to make sure she will be available when you need her services quickly. It's a fun lunch, freely mixing personal and professional information.

(continued on next page...)

Looking for a new challenge? The Vault Finance Job Board has
thousands of top jobs for all experience levels. Visit www.vault.com.

VAULT   35

A Day in the Life of A Venture Capitalist (cont'd)

2:00   Call new companies you have heard about over the last few days. Ideally you could do this task a little bit every day, but you find you need to be in a friendly and upbeat mood to make these calls, so you batch them. Also, if you actually get in touch with the CEO, you may be on the phone for 90 minutes, so you need to have an open block of time. You leave the standard pitch about your firm on the voice mail of the CEO's of four other companies. You get through to one CEO, and although you can tell in the first five minutes that you won't be interested in investing, you talk for 30 minutes. You spend most of the 30 minutes probing about competitors who might be better than the company you're talking to and finding out more about his market space.

3:00   You and a partner meet with a portfolio company on a conference call. The company is facing some challenges and you offer to screen executive recruiters to help find a new CFO for it. The GP offers to talk to two M&A firms to get a first opinion about what might be done to sell the company over the next six months. At the end of the call, the GP gives you three names and numbers of recruiters, which you add to your own two contacts.

3:30   You call the recruiters, explaining the situation and asking about their recent experiences in similar searches. The critical element is whether the recruiters actually have time and interest in doing the search. You talk to two recruiters and leave voice mails for the other three.

4:30   You make due diligence calls for a potential investment you have been following for two months. Last week you called the company's customers, and they seemed happy for the most part. Today, you are calling the personal references of the management team. The idea is to get as much negative information as possible. You need to discover any potential character or personality flaws any member of the team may have. VC firms are "due diligence machines," doing the hard work of making sure a company is what it says it is.

5:30	You make calls to the West Coast. You also check your stocks and confirm dinner plans. You do some miscellaneous surfing on the Web to gather some articles about the technology areas you cover.
6:30	You stand around the halls talking with other members of your firm, brainstorming and filling each other in about what's happening in your area.
7:00	Dinner with two other young VCs downtown. You talk mostly about life, sports, travel and relationships, but also about the latest deals, cool business ideas, and recent successes. You find out that a competing firm just made 30 times their money on a deal you never saw. You also find out that a company you turned down which was invested in by someone else is about to go bankrupt. A train missed; a bullet dodged.

Career path

There is no typical path for a successful career in venture capital. There are, however, three main paths.

The first path is the least common. Out of college or after two years at a management consulting firm or investment bank, or after graduating from business school, a person is hired as an analyst or associate at a venture capital firm. Sometimes, business school grads are hired as associates, senior associates or vice presidents. After two to six years, successful associates are invited to become principals or partners. How long it takes to move up depends on your performance and the rate of growth of the venture firm. If the firm is growing quickly, it is often faster and less risky for the firm to promote young associates than to bring in experienced hires.

The second path, to be hired by a VC firm as an experienced professional in information technology, health services, or biotech, is more common. After two to six years (normally after attending business school), these hires are invited to become a principal or partner.

Finally, successful entrepreneurs may be asked to join a venture firm as a partner in their 30s or 40s.

Looking for a new challenge? The Vault Finance Job Board has thousands of top jobs for all experience levels. Visit www.vault.com.

VAULT 37

In all cases, once someone is a partner, the percent of the "carry" (profits) they receive increases the longer they stay at the firm and the more important their investments have been to the profitability of the firm.

Pay & Perks

Venture capital firms offer unique types of compensation. They are:

Closing Bonus: A bonus is often given to lower-level employees for sourcing or doing due diligence when an investment is closed. Most early stage firms do not give this lower-level bonus, although some, like Summitt Partners and Battery Ventures, do. This bonus is intended to focus their attention on the best deals and work hard to get them closed.

Co-investment: This common perk allows VCs to invest their own money alongside the firm in some deals. If a firm is successful, the upside of co-investment can far exceed salary and bonuses.

Carry: A percentage of the profits the firm makes. Carry is the Holy Grail of venture capital. A senior associate might get 0.25 to 0.5 percent initially. A Partner might start with 0.5 percent and move to 4 percent over his/her career. Example: if a firm has a $100 million fund and triples it over 8 years, profit might be $200 million. A 1 percent carry would thus be worth $2 million dollars.

The following are very general salary figures for the venture capital industry:

Analyst: Salary $45,000 - $70,000. Annual Bonus $15,000. Closing Bonus, Yes. Co-investment, No.

Associate: Salary $80,000 - $120,000. Annual Bonus $50,000. Closing Bonus, Yes. Co-investment, Yes. Carry, sometimes a small amount.

Sr. Associate/VP: Salary $150,000. Bonus $150,000. Closing Bonus, Yes. Co-investment, Yes. Carry, probably.

Partner: Salary $200,000 - $300,000. Annual Bonus $500,000. Closing Bonus, No. Co-investment, Yes. Carry, Yes.

Perks of Working in Venture Capital

1. You often get to be the one making decisions because you have money.

2. Over the long term, you will certainly become rich because the job is well paying and you should eventually get "carry" or equity in the firm.

3. Being "in the middle of it all" in some of the most interesting industries.

4. You have access to the best minds — the people you work with are typically very smart and interesting.

5. Your job is to absorb and enjoy the positive creative energy of entrepreneurs and direct it toward successful execution.

6. You could suddenly become rich if one of your companies does extremely well and you were able to co-invest or you have carry.

7. You have access to the best information systems.

Negatives of Working in Venture Capital

Because the venture capital industry is "the hot thing," people often forget to question whether it is the right job for them. Here is a list of some of the negatives we hear from people who have worked in the industry for a while.

1. You don't have pride of ownership in anything. You're just an investor, not a builder.

2. VC is a slow path to wealth compared with the immediate cash income you get in investment banking, hedge funds or even management consulting.

3. You are a jack-of-all-trades, not an expert. After a few years, you can't do anything other than VC because you grow spoiled by making decisions without much compromise.

4. Venture capital is fundamentally a negative process. Because you reject 99 of every 100 plans, year after year, over time you focus on figuring out what is wrong with a company so you can reject it and get onto the next deal. What is wrong with the management? The technology? The deal terms? The strategy? After just a few years, that mentality may bleed into your life. What is wrong with my partners? What is wrong with my spouse? What is wrong with me? Oh, the angst!

5. Because you reject 99 of every 100 entrepreneurs, you make a lot of enemies, no matter how nice and helpful you try to be. No one likes rejection, and passionate entrepreneurs have long memories.

Looking for a new challenge? The Vault Finance Job Board has thousands of top jobs for all experience levels. Visit www.vault.com.

VAULT 39

Lifestyle

Hours

Venture capitalists typically work at least 60 to 70 hours per week. (It takes a lot of effort to keep your edge.) The VC community is still a small one. Networking and having the informational edge are vital to VC career success. All of this takes time, especially at the beginning of your career when you're just building a reputation.

Dress

Increasingly, venture capitalists are opting for business casual garb. For one, VCs don't need to dress to impress – they're the ones with the money. Venture capitalists also work extensively with high-tech entrepreneurs, who are normally casually dressed (to say the least). (You'll see a surprising number of Timex watches.)

Diversity

Diversity is a serious issue to the venture community. There are very few women and very few African-Americans in the industry. It's always hard to say why one industry moves more quickly or slowly in this regard than another, but it seems venture capital has moved slowly because of the confidence issue. For everyone in this wealth creation chain – the entrepreneur, the VC, the investment bank, the press – guessing which companies will succeed is very difficult and picking wrong has a serious impact on the bottom line. As a default, most people move to a mode of "pattern recognition." If they see a management team, business model or market position they have made money with before, they tend to choose it. Race and gender are factors that people "pattern recognize" as well. In a high-risk business, white men look safer – unfair though this may be.

Many venture firms have been trying to address the issue of diversity. In the end, if you are a woman or an ethnic minority, you need to do what everyone else needs to do: become an expert in an industry, show good judgement, and schmooze.

How Do You Spot A Good Investment?

If this could be definitively answered, venture capital would be a secure business indeed! Many of the most successful companies were rejected by multiple VC firms. And many companies that have received $10 million, $40 million, and even $400 million in venture capital money have disappeared.

The "perfect investment" has:

1. A complete management team with experience and integrity who you enjoy spending time with. They are loved by their employees, and they are savvy with the investment community.

2. A clearly defined, large and unexploited market opportunity.

3. A finished product that works.

4. A set of customers with money to spend.

5. A product that serves a clear need.

6. A company that is located in a place where it is easily monitored.

7. A low price.

8. No other institutional investors, or excellent early stage investors.

9. A leading position in the targeted market.

10. A unique set of capabilities that will keep the company ahead of the competition, with or without patents.

Other opportunities are "hairy," displaying some element of risk. But what doesn't?

Looking for a new challenge? The Vault Finance Job Board has
thousands of top jobs for all experience levels. Visit www.vault.com.

VAULT   41

Final Analysis

Venture capital is a unique field in the business world – combining elements of play (which fledgling startup will blossom into a player? Place your bets!) with deadly seriousness (can you be the first one to invest in the next Federal Express or eBay?) If you think you have the insight to choose wisely, the charm and contacts to obtain information and the endurance to work hard constantly, then join the crowds considering venture capital. The industry coming off of a significant "peak" and as it goes through two to three years of a down cycle, the VC job market is going to be even tougher. If you really want to do it, patience and persistence are a **must**. In today's environment, it could take a year or more to identify and secure an opportunity, even with the proper background. The rewards, of course, both intellectually and financially, can be worth it.

Looking for a new challenge? The Vault Finance Job Board has thousands of top jobs for all experience levels. Visit www.vault.com.

V/\ULT   43

Glossary

Carry: A percentage of the profits the firm makes. Carry is the Holy Grail of venture capital. Typically, the general partners receive a combined 20 percent of the profit from investing. For instance, if a firm receives $100 million in capital for its fund, and over 10 years returns $400 million, the profit was $300 million. The investors, or limited partners, receive 80 percent or $240 million, and the general partners split 20 percent or $60 million among themselves. Some premier VC firms have reportedly raised carry to 30 percent.

Closing: After the due diligence is done, and the VC finally decides to invest in the company, there is a legal closing of the deal. Involving lawyers and large contracts, the process can take one to four weeks.

Co-investment: A common program through which employees can invest their own money alongside the firm in some or all of the portfolio companies. If a firm is successful, the upside to this program can far exceed the salary and bonuses.

Closing bonus: A bonus often given to lower-level employees for sourcing or doing due diligence on deals that are done. This is intended to focus their attention on the best deals and work hard to get them closed.

Crater: A company that received venture capital and subsequently went bankrupt.

Dog: A company that received venture capital but is failing or going nowhere. "You can combine a dog with another dog, but you're still going to have a dog."

Due diligence: The process of investigating a company before investing in it. It typically includes calling references, calling customers, investigating competitors, validating legal contracts, visiting remote locations, coordinating with other investors, interviewing the entire management team, testing the technology, building spreadsheets and running sensitivity analyses on the projections to see if they make sense, etc.

Entrepreneur-in-residence: see Venture partner.

Looking for a new challenge? The Vault Finance Job Board has thousands of top jobs for all experience levels. Visit www.vault.com.

VAULT   45

Exit: This is an event, or series of events, that allows a VC firm to turn the equity it owns in a company back into cash. That event is usually a sale of the company to a larger company, or an IPO that permits the firm to sell its shares. Typically, the VC cannot exit at the time of an IPO because they are "locked up" by the investment banks executing the IPO [see "lock up"]

Fund: The pool of money a venture capital firm raises to invest. The money is typically committed by the limited partners for a period of 10 years. The money does not sit in a bank account for ten years. In practice, the money is "drawn down" by the general partners as they need it for investments they are pursuing. Thus, most of the money stays with the limited partners, earning whatever rate of return they can achieve, until it is transferred to the VC for investment within a few weeks.

General partner: A partner in a VC firm. The person making the investment decisions and sitting on the boards of portfolio companies.

IPO: Initial Public Offering. Also known as "going public." When a company first issues equity shares for purchase by the public on one of the public exchanges.

IRR: Internal Rate of Return. A calculation that determines the rate of return on a portfolio investment or on the total venture fund. If, for example, you put your money in a bank account that gives you 5.5 percent interest annually, you could say your IRR on that investment would be roughly 5.5 percent (not accounting for taxes or service fees). IRR is the most important measure of performance for a VC fund.

Limited partner: An investor in a VC fund. Typically pension funds, endowments, wealthy individuals, and strategic investors such as large corporations which want access to the young companies in the VC's portfolio.

Limited partnership: The legal structure of many venture capital firms. It protects the investors in the fund from legal responsibility for things the fund managers might do. It also protects the partners by interference by investors for the duration of the fund, typically 10 years.

Lock-up: In an IPO, the venture capital firm is "locked-up" for a period of three to 18 months by the investment banks executing the public offering. The VC firm is not allowed to sell shares on the public market.

The reason for the lock-up? The market might see the VC selling shares as a negative signal. The job of the investment bank is to manage an orderly process that won't spook the market and have an adverse effect on the share price. Banks therefore get VCs to agree to a reasonable lock-up period.

Management fee: The general partners take a percentage of the fund every year to pay for expenses. Typically, a firm will charge the fund 2.5 percent. This pays for salaries, office space, travel, computers, phones, advertising, and legal expenses.

Partnership: Short for limited partnership.

Pre-money valuation: Value of the company before a VC invests capital. If, for example, a VC invests $2 million in a company and subsequently owns 25 percent of the company, then the pre-money value must have been $6 million. ($2/X = .25$. X thus equals 8, and since we know the VC firm added $2 million of value, the company must have been worth $8 – $2 = $6 million "pre-money.")

Post-money valuation: The value of the company after a VC invests capital. Example: if a VC invests $2 million in a company and subsequently owns 25 percent, the post-money valuation must have been $8 million. The VC added $2 million of value (now cash in the company's bank account) so $2/X=.25$. X= $8 million.

SBIC: Small Business Investment Corporation. The U.S. Federal Government program that provides matching funds to venture capital firms to augment the amount they have available to invest. The SBIC program was created by the Small Business Investment Act of 1958. The Small Business Administration ("SBA") is the administrator for the program and is responsible for licensing SBICs. The program recognizes the efficacy of having private individuals, not the government, investing money in entrepreneurial ventures. Traditionally, venture funds that receive SBIC money have been considered lower-tier investors. That perception may be changing.

Sourcing: The process of finding investment opportunities. The person in a venture firm who does this well is very valuable to a firm. Because a deal may sometimes come from multiple sources simultaneously, there is often politicking within a VC firm to be credited with bringing a deal in the door.

Looking for a new challenge? The Vault Finance Job Board has thousands of top jobs for all experience levels. Visit www.vault.com.

VAULT   47

This is especially true when there is a bonus given for sourcing a deal that receives funding.

Term sheet: A generally non-binding document prepared by a venture capital company detailing the conditions of investment to an entreprenuer. The term sheet covers the fundamental provisions of an investment and is often negotiated. Typical items in a term sheet include percentage of ownership, monetary investment and changes to a company's charter and bylaws.

Venture partner: An aspiring entrepreneur invited by a VC to hang out in their offices, use the phone, and use their networks to flesh out a business plan and build a management team. The VC will then provide initial funding to the venture. It's a way for a VC to build proprietary deal flow, and insure they are investing in the best entrepreneurs. It also helps the entrepreneurs by giving them a safe and credible place from which to investigate their ideas.

About the Author

Anita Kapadia graduated from New York University's Stern School of Business with a BS in Finance and holds an MFA from Columbia in creative writing. Anita previously worked as an investment banking analyst at Merrill Lynch.

James Currier is a nine-year veteran of the venture capital industry and a student of its evolving nature. He was introduced to the business in 1991 by GTE New Ventures in California, and spent three years at Battery Ventures in Boston through 1997. While at Battery, Currier co-founded "Capital Venture", the association of young venture capitalists. Currier is a graduate of Princeton University (1990) and of Harvard Business School (1999).

Looking for a new challenge? The Vault Finance Job Board has thousands of top jobs for all experience levels. Visit www.vault.com.

VAULT   49

Coca-Cola acquires Mad River Traders Inc. 5/11/01

Classic Communications to borrow $75 million in senior bank debt from CSFB and Brera Capital Partners. 5/10/01

Kraft Foods hopes to raise as much as $8.7 billion in an IPO. 5/2/01

Procter & Gamble is turned down in $4-4.5 billion bid for Clairol. 5/11/01

Gavitec GmbH received an undisclosed amount of investment capital from Gold-Zack AG. 5/10/01

Multiplex Inc. landed $105 million from several top investment banks, including JP Morgan. 5/10/01

Zhone Technologies withdrew its $345 million IPO. 5/8/01

US Timberlands receives $106 buyout offer from senior management. 5/14/01

Imperial Tobacco buys 75% stake in Tobaccor. 4/2/01

Facing bankruptcy due to its more than $1.5 billion in debt, Teligent will lay off 38% of its workforce. 5/14/01

AB Barrandov a.s. for sale for $33.3 million. MGM, Paramount possibly interested. 5/14/01

Veronis Suhler buys Phillips Business Information and Hart Publishing from Phillips International for over $100 million. 10/4/00

SED. FINALLY, A DAILY PAPER FOR THE OBSESSED. FINF

We're as obsessed with deals as you are. We report more deals every week, and in more detail, than any other business publication. The only way to get The Daily Deal is to subscribe: Call us now at 1-888-667-DEAL, email: subs@TheDeal.com, or visit us at TheDeal.com. **If you're missing The Deal, you're missing deals.**

Increase your T/NJ Ratio
(Time to New Job)

Use the Internet's most targeted
job search tools for finance
professionals.

Vault Finance Job Board

The most comprehensive and convenient job board for finance
professionals. Target your search by area of finance, function,
and experience level, and find the job openings that you want.
No surfing required.

VaultMatch Resume Database

Vault takes match-making to the next level: post your resume
and customize your search by area of finance, experience and
more. We'll match job listings with your interests and criteria
and e-mail them directly to your in-box.

VAULT
> the insider career network™